Intricate Design Coloring Book Two

Mary Ann Seymour

Printed by Create Space, An Amazon.com Company

Available from Amazon.com, Create Space.com and other online stores

Preface

This book is dedicated to all the people who have encouraged me to press on. It has been a time of great testing, during which I have learned a great deal. Thus, it has also been a time of learning to lean into the Lord and learning to trust Him more fully. I want to thank Tamara Lowe for all the education I received in her school, <u>Kingdom Builders Academy</u>. I know that without it I would not be writing this preface. I Also wish to thank Dayna Belcher for her support and for all the encouragement of friends on Facebook who were there for me through it all. I would not forget my family, or my family at Family of Faith Community Church. I want to encourage each of you to stir up your giftings regardless of your age. You are not too old to see your dreams come true. Don't wait until you are eighty-three years old as I did. Do it now. Ask the Father for help to meet your goals. He will walk with you through it.

This being said: Enjoy yourself this pleasure. Life passes quickly and we look back and wish that we had spent more time soaking up the pleasures God has provided for us.

The Challenge Continues.

If you own book one, you know that intricate means that it is difficult and challenging. If you do not have book one, you will quickly find that this book is for those who want to stretch their abilities. So if you are up for a real challenge, this is the book for you. So put on your creative ability. You will find enjoyment and satisfaction in conquering the challenge, and you will also have a beautiful piece of art work.

Go on, pick up those colored pencils and color some of these. You know you want to. You know you do! Remember how you used to color when you were younger?

Why you would want to color:

- You want something different to do.
- You like a challenge.
- You love color.
- You loved to color when you were younger.
- Science has proven that coloring is a stress relieving, relaxing therapy.
- It is an activity you can share with your children.
- It is an activity you can do when the electricity is off and there is no TV, or other electronic devices working!
- The worrisome thoughts that you have had will be forgotten as you concentrate on which colors to use and where to us them.

Add some soothing music to that and you have a winning combination.

You will find some pictures quite easy to color. Others will be a real challenge. I wanted to try something different, so I added some that have added shading. Some have dark lines and light lines. If coloring the smaller sections with the light lines is too much of a challenge, just color over them. Don't feel as though you must color ever space. I think they look nice with some white spaces.

I believe that you will enjoy this book. I hope so. I have enjoyed making the designs. Putting it together was not the part I enjoyed most. I just wanted to keep making more designs. So, I decided to make book two.

May your joy be full as you color the pages in this book.

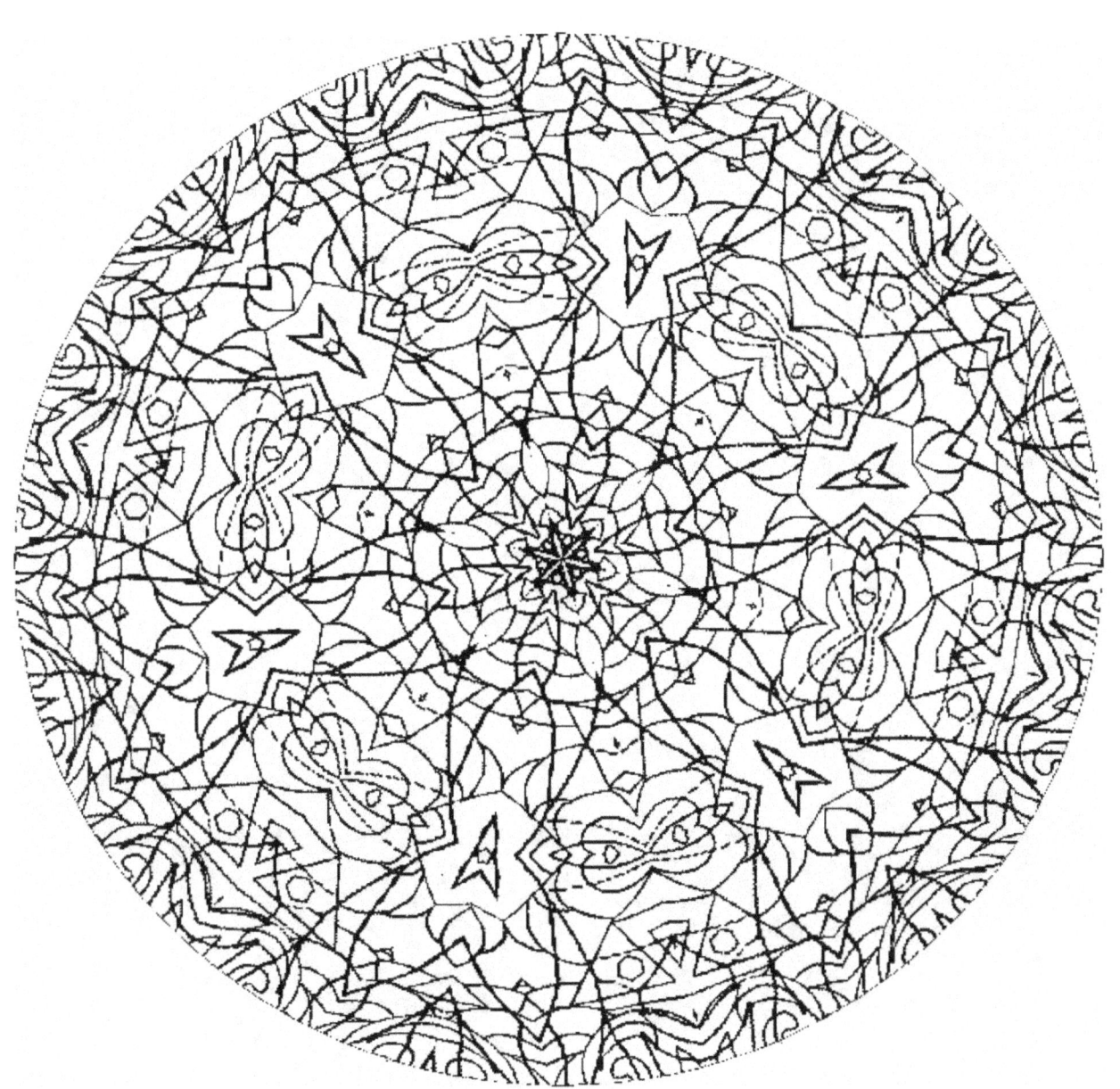

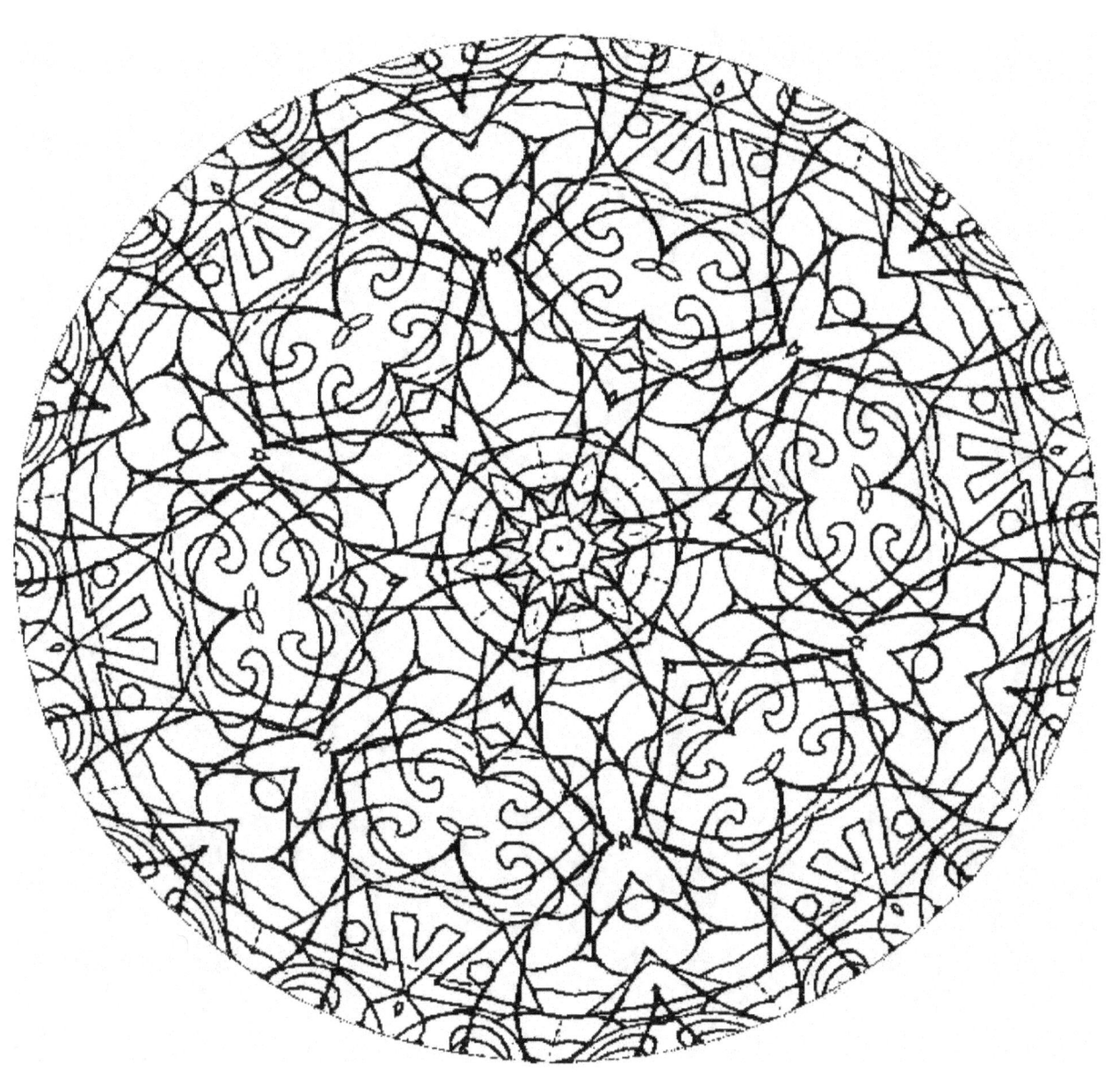

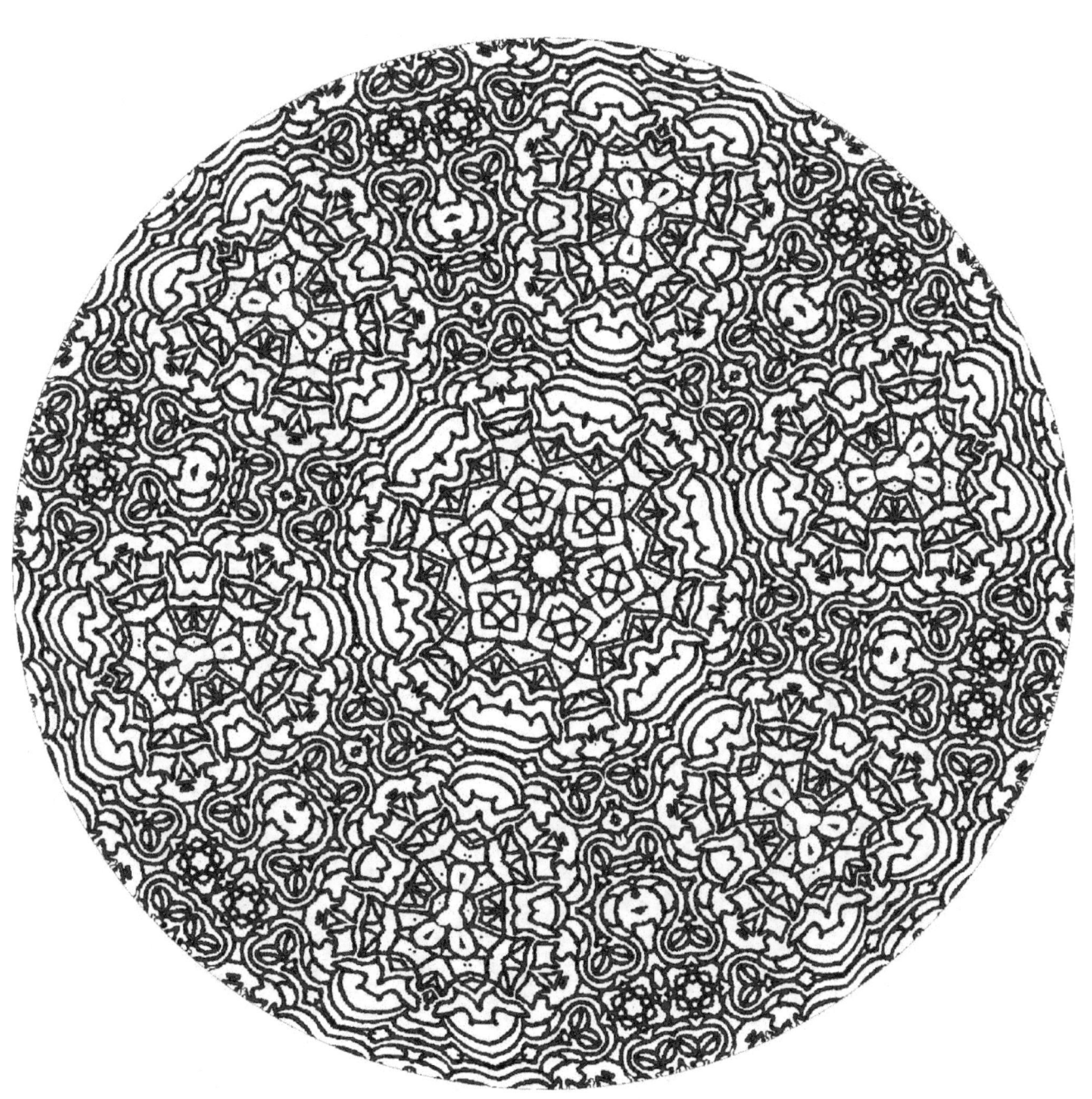

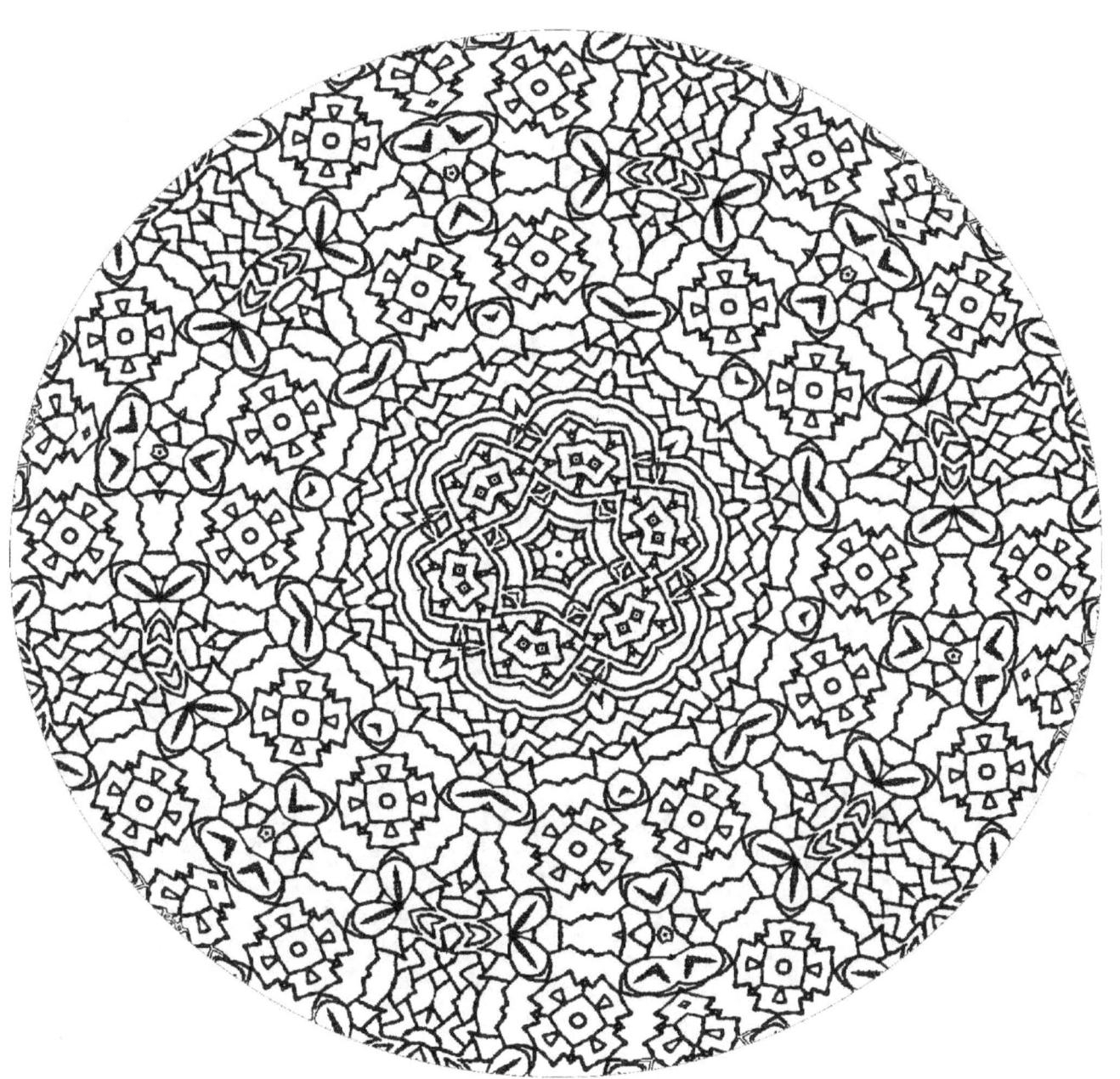

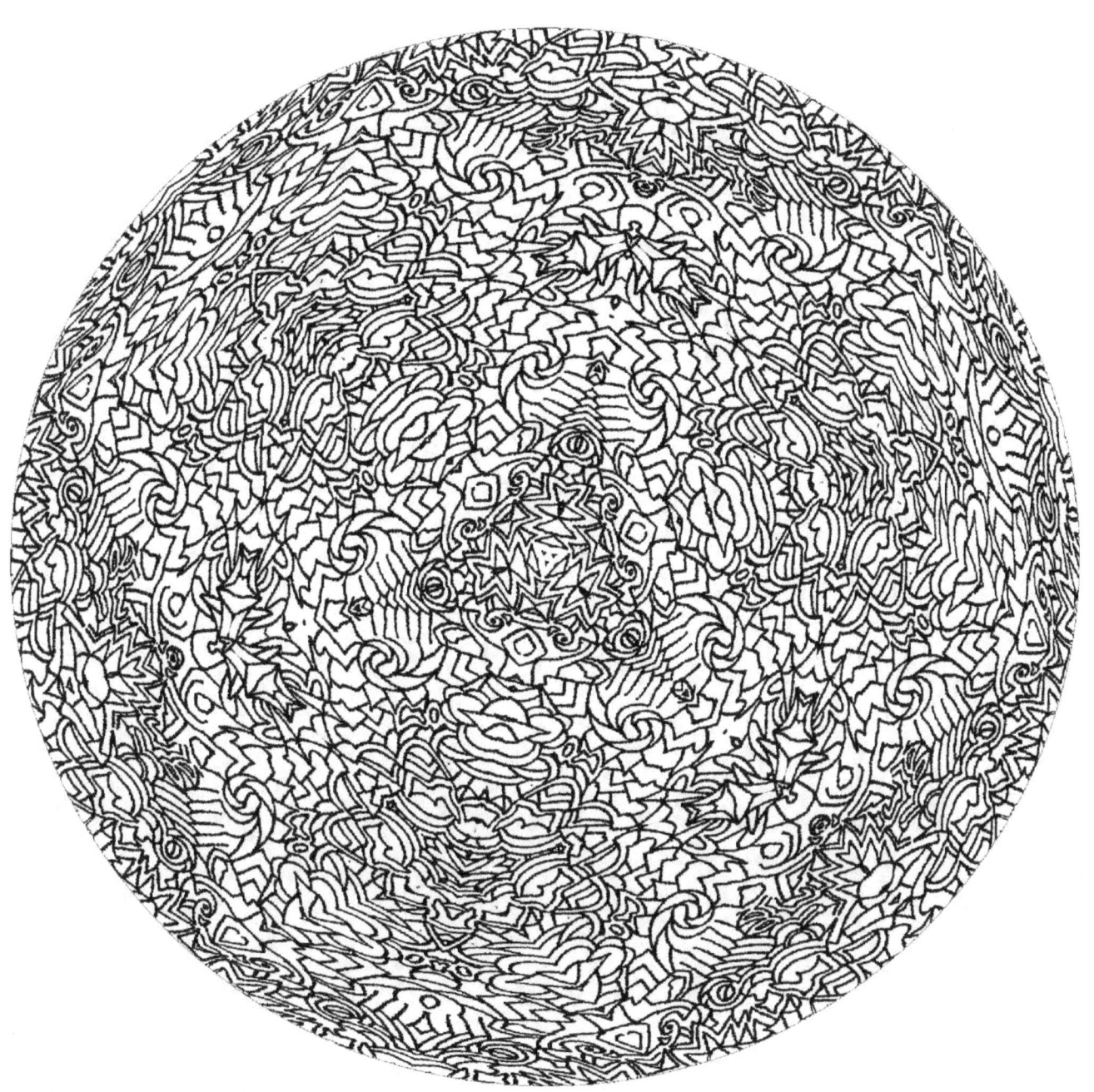

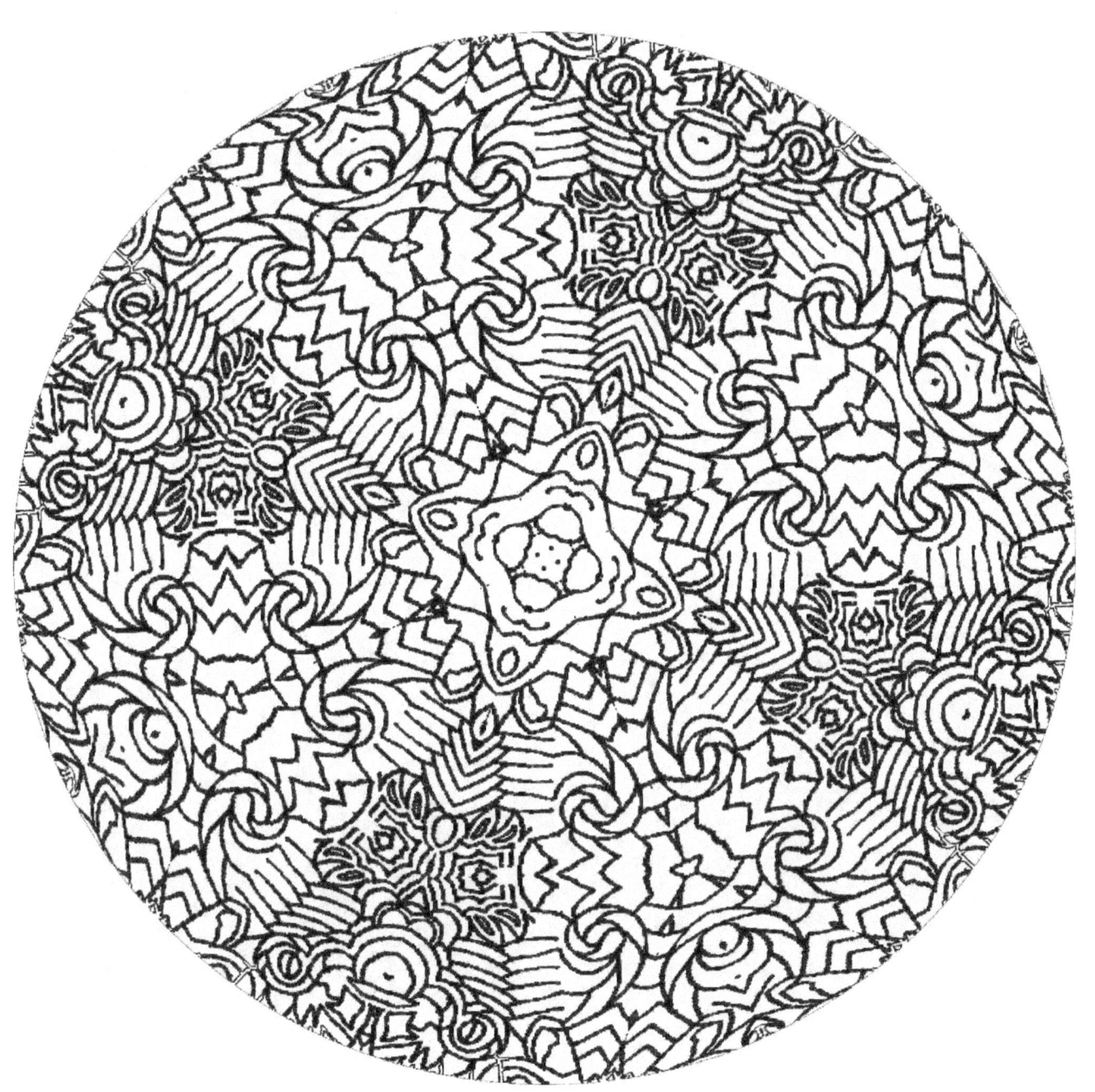

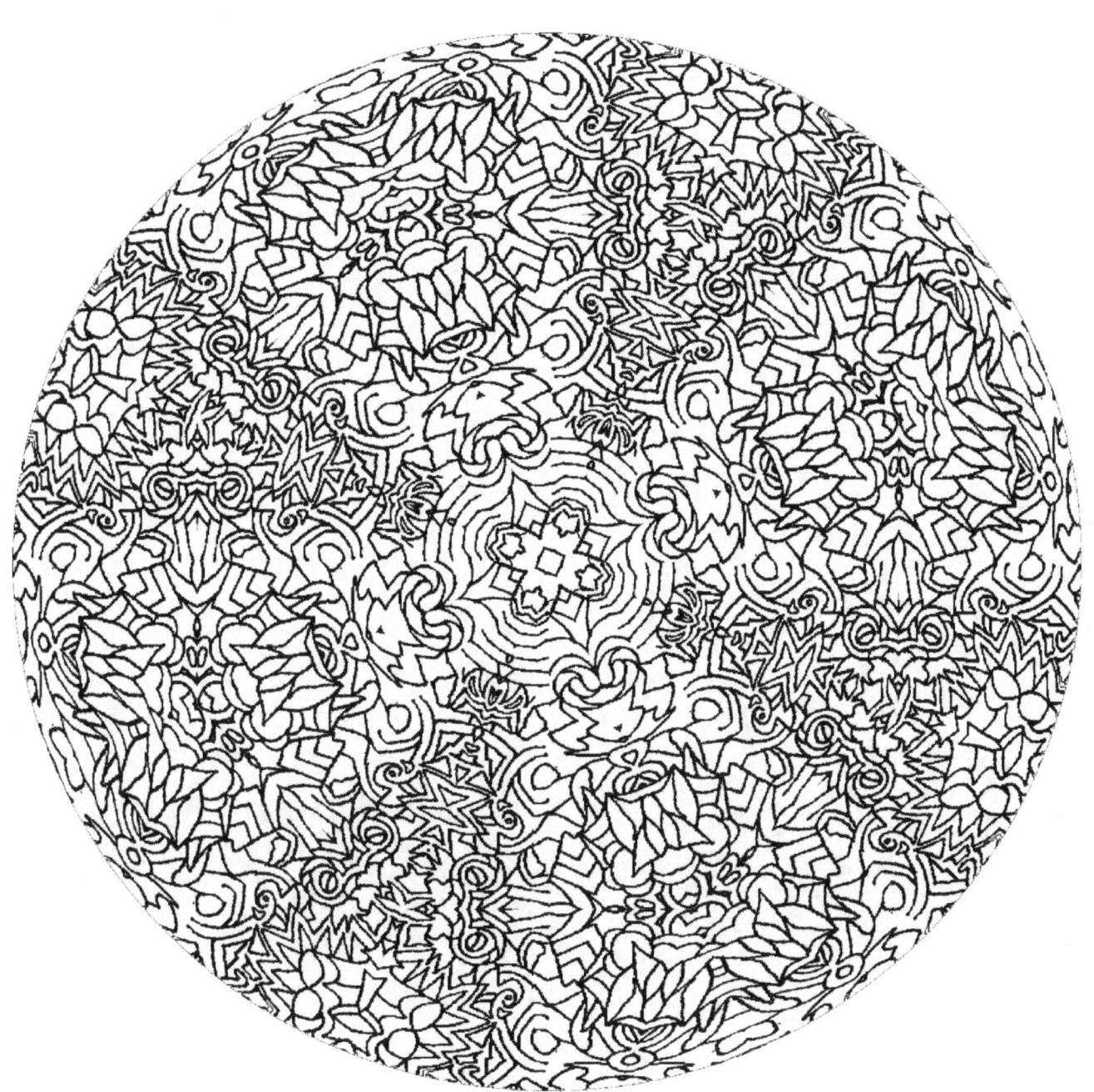

About the Designer

Mary Ann does not claim to be an artist, but she says that, if, given a pencil, an eraser as long as a pencil, as well as a picture to look at, she can at times, draw something that looks, just a little like the original. However, she does like to doodle, and from that developed the ability to make coloring designs. She also likes to use software to produce beautiful fractal designs which she prints out and frames, and/or shrinks and puts into jewelry. She also likes to make colored kaleidoscope designs and kaleidoscope designs that move. She hopes to soon have some of these products for sale on line. Intricate Coloring Book Two will soon be on its way. Look for it. Blessings to all.

www.ingramcontent.com/pod-product-compliance
Lightning Source LLC
Chambersburg PA
CBHW081354280526

45788CB00009B/2875